Criminology

Top 10 Famous Cases Discovered By Crime Psychology

Copyright © 2020

DEDICATION

Contents

Hannibal Lecter

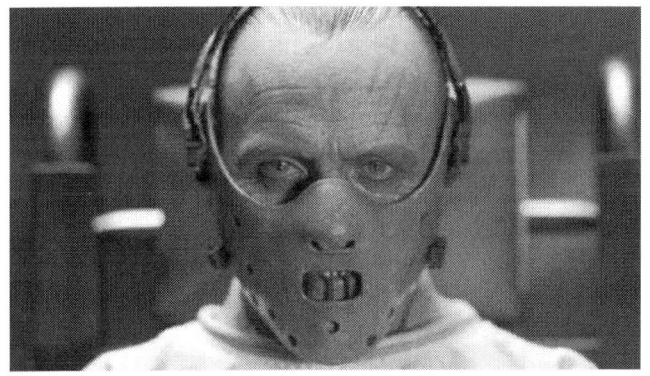

HANNIBAL LECTER: A SYMPATHETIC VICTIM

"To know all is to forgive all."

In The Silence of the Lambs, the character of Hannibal Lecter dismisses the possibility that his crimes can be explained, defiantly boasting, "Nothing happened to me ... I happened. You can't reduce me to a set of influences" (Harris, 1988, p. 20). Yet in spite of all Lecter's existential bravado, a passage in one of Harris' subsequent books suggests that something did happen to him, and he can be reduced to a set of influences. In Hannibal (Harris, 1999), Lecter falls asleep on an airplane. Dreaming, he recalls a terrible episode from World War II: his aristocrat parents were

1

murdered by deserters from the wartime front. The children of the estate were locked in a barn, and when the famished deserters depleted their food supply, they came for the children. Like something derived from the story of Hansel and Gretel (Tatar, 2004), the deserters palpated Hannibal's thigh, arm, and chest, but instead selected his younger sister, Mischa. Young Lecter clung tightly to her, but the men slammed a barn door on him, cracking the bone in his upper arm. Young Hannibal released her and Mischa was led away, ostensibly "to play," but even from the barn, Lecter could still hear the sound of the axe. Later, he recognized her teeth in the reeking pit that his captives used as a toilet.

Several other commentators have located the etiology of Lecter's crimes in this traumatic event (Hannibal Lecter, 2005; Hannibal Library, 2005; Hawker, 2001). For example, Bruno (2005) has explored the link between the Mischa account and Hannibal's crimes, writing:

Mischa's horrible slaughter and consumption by the deserters formed the fantasy that shaped Hannibal Lecter, a revenge fantasy. In his dream, the deserters are crude and uncouth. They're not soldiers but deserters, cowards, ignoble by definition. They take over Lecter's parents' property and relegate the young residents to the barn. Their breath stinks. They butcher a deer as Neanderthals

2

would. They screech like greedy vultures when they see the spilled blood seeping into the snow. When he grows up, Lecter targets men he considered petty and uncouth. Raspail the inferior flutist, Krendler the vindictive bureaucrat, Pazzi the corrupt cop, the census taker, even Mason Verger the former libertine who managed by a miracle of medical science to survive Lecter's wrath — all of them are nothing more than stand-ins for the deserters who ate his sister.

While Bruno's explanation goes quite a long way in making Lecter's monstrous offenses understandable, even heroic, the death of Mischa does not explain all of Lecter's crimes. It does not, for example, explain his attack on FBI Agent Will Graham (Harris, 1981). Graham, after all, is no cretin. Lecter views him as a fellow professional. In fact, stating, "The reason you caught me is that we're just alike," Lecter suggests that he believes Graham is a kindred spirit. Similarly, the avenging of Mischa's death cannot explain the murder of two police officers that were assigned to guard Lecter (Harris, 1988), or the disfiguring attack on a hospital nurse (Harris, 1981). Mischa's death does, however, make Lecter a far more sympathetic figure (Picart & Greek, 2003) and provide a facile explanation for Lecter's cannibalism – a paradoxical sort of cannibalism that violates the most primal of taboos while simultaneously showing off Lecter's status as a member of the haute monde (Oleson, 2005). Bruno (2005) continues:

Obviously he eats his victims because they ate Mischa. An eye for an eye. But why the gourmet preparation? Why serve their organs sautéed in butter and shallots? Why spend exorbitant amounts of money on vintage wines to go with these human entrees? Because Lecter knows he's better than the troglodytes who killed his sister. He has refinement and a noble lineage. He would never eat meat roasted on a stick. He does it the most sophisticated way possible. His meticulous preparation of human flesh is his way of throwing it in the faces of the deserters who gnawed on Mischa's bones.

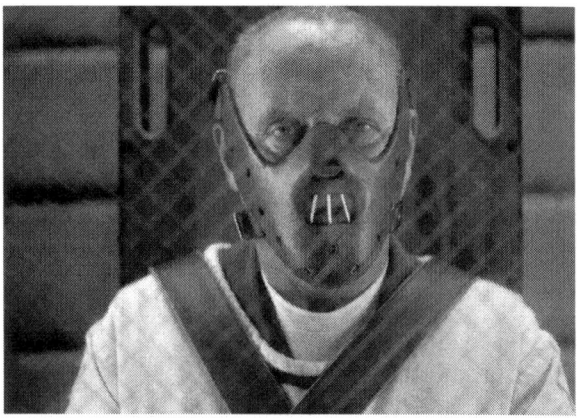

This, however, is a disappointingly pedestrian explanation for the crimes of such a grand villain. Critic Roger Ebert has suggested that film characters are far more compelling when they retain an air of mystery than when they are explained away with shorthand Freud (Simpson, 2000). Perhaps author Thomas Harris found himself in the same position as English poet John Milton, who "wrote in fetters when he wrote of Angels and God, and at liberty when of Devils and Hell [...] because he was a true Poet and of the Devil's party without knowing it". Perhaps, having created a villain who was so skillfully drawn that he appeared heroic, Thomas Harris felt the need to invent some kind of exculpatory deus ex machina that would allow Hannibal Lecter to serve as his protagonist (in Hannibal) rather than as a compelling-but-wicked antagonist (in Red Dragon and The Silence of the Lambs). Yet with the unveiling of the story of Mischa, the character of Lecter has lost a great deal of his mystique. Under this interpretation, Hannibal Lecter is no monster, no vampire, and no devil — instead, he is nothing more than a victim, a vigilante, a Deathwish Charles Bronson with a fondness for the Oxford English Dictionary and an appetite for forbidden food. Any keen undergraduate with a copy of Hannibal and a basic psychology primer could explain away Lecter's crimes. The parallels between Mischa's death and Lecter's crimes are so obvious that it requires a willful kind of blindness not to arrive at the conclusions articulated by Bruno (2005). Thus, unless he is blinded by a profound state of denial, Dr. Hannibal Lecter, a world-class psychiatrist with an

5

immeasurably high IQ score, should be well aware of the parallels between his sister's death and his own crimes. And if he is aware of the parallels, Lecter was lying through his cannibalistic teeth when he gloated that he could not be reduced to a set of influences. According to the Mischa story, Lecter is a set of influences, and almost nothing else.

It is not only keen undergraduates who have attempted to explain the forces that make Lecter tick. Academics, too, have dissected the psyche of Hannibal Lecter, and located the origins of Lecter's crimes in the trauma of his childhood. Messent (2000), for example, claims that Lecter's crimes are a form of repetitive compulsion, stemming from the brutal murder of his sister. Gregory (2002) argues that Lecter suffers from post-traumatic stress disorder, and notes that, analyzed from an object-relations perspective, Lecter is in a paranoid-schizoid position, relying heavily upon schizoid defenses. Through his relationship with Starling, however, he enters into the depressive position. Reductive psychology appears to explain Dr. Lecter handily (Dery, 1999; Whitty, 2002). Lecter is not the irreducible riddle that he pretends to be. Rather, he is explainable, intelligible, and ultimately distillable to a set of obvious influences. His murders, his avenging cannibalism, his fascination with string theory (through which he hopes to reverse time and restore Mischa to the world), and even his relationship with Clarice Starling (whom he views as a re-emergence of Mischa) all stem from the same overwhelming need to undo his sister's death. Viewed through the lens of the Mischa story, Lecter is not a monstrous killer – he is a hero, using his prodigious intellect and superhuman talents to seek a single goal: the restoration of his murdered sister to the world.

But not everyone believes that Lecter should have been transformed from a monstrous villain into a hero. The actor Jodie Foster reportedly said that Harris "betrayed" the character of Starling by uniting her with Lecter in the final pages of Hannibal (Lambs 'in doubt', 2000). It was, in her eyes, a disappointment. But Hannibal (Harris, 1999) is not only disappointing in a literary sense; it is also deeply disappointing from a criminological point of view. It is disappointing because the Mischa story effectively moots an important criminological question. If Lecter's cannibalistic murders are merely inverted reenactments of Mischa's murder, Lecter's behavior can be explained with elementary psychology. If Lecter's crimes are nothing more than the mathematical culmination of his traumatic childhood experiences, the books have little practical value to offer the social scientist. But if the character of Hannibal Lecter is correct when he states that "We don't invent our natures ... [and that] they're issued to us along with our lungs and pancreas and everything else" (Harris, 1981, p. 241), another explanation must be sought to explain why a genius – a man of medicine, an urbane polymath – would deliberately choose to kill and consume another human being. It very well may be the case that Lecter's crimes are something more than clumsily-inverted reenactments, and more than the summation of his influences. But if there is more to Lecter's crimes than a repetition of childhood trauma, then criminologists must ask if another explanation exists, and must squarely face the question of whether moral evil can be a legitimate explanation for criminal behavior.

HANNIBAL LECTER: VICTIM OF EVIL FORCES

"The problem of evil is still with us ... except that of attributing evil to Satan, we look for the demonic figures in the world around us."

It was suggested above that Hannibal Lecter may be a victim who, because of the traumatic events that haunt him, was destined by experience to become a cannibalistic serial killer. But perhaps it was not Lecter's experiences that compelled him to kill, but a malignancy of his soul. Perhaps it was Lecter's fundamental nature — not his nurture — that destined him to murder. The origins of Hannibal Lecter's terrible crimes may be rooted not in the trauma of his childhood, but in something akin to metaphysical evil.

Is the character of Hannibal Lecter evil? Author Harris does not provide the reader with a clean and unambiguous answer in the text of the novels. Instead, he forces his readers to wrestle with moral descriptions that are difficult to navigate, for example describing Lecter as both "good and terrible" in Hannibal (Harris, 1999, p. 87). Worthy of particular note is an exchange in which Harris plays upon the irreconcilable tension between "scientific" and "theological" explanations for Lecter's crimes. In The Silence of the Lambs, Hannibal Lecter "waves away the idea of a psychological explanation, a cause, a motive" (Hawker, 2001) for his crimes, and dares the character of FBI Agent Clarice Starling to consider the possibility that he is metaphysically evil. He taunts, "You've given up good and evil for behaviorism, Officer Starling. You've got everybody in moral dignity pants – nothing is ever anybody's fault. Look at me Officer Starling. Can you stand to say I'm evil? Am I evil?".

Agent Starling cannot bring herself to label Lecter as "evil" and instead suggests that he has been "destructive" (Harris, 1988, p. 20). While Starling's inability to condemn Lecter as evil may merely have been good manners (i.e., not calling Lecter a name to his face), the inability to identify a cannibalistic serial killer as "evil" appears to be proof of Delbanco's (1995) claim that Americans have lost their ability to recognize real evil, even when it stands directly before them. If serial murder and cannibalism are not evil, then what is?

The answer to Lecter's seemingly simple question – "Am I evil?" – should be of great interest to criminologists. In all likelihood, the answer depends upon the working definition of "evil" that is employed. A number of approaches exist, since the concept of evil has been studied from many disciplinary perspectives over time (Hedgehog Review, 2000). For example, sociologists view evil – wholly or in part – as the result of social forces that shape and misshape individuals and institutions in society. Similarly, psychologists focus on the minds and the mental states of individuals who have committed evil deeds, while legal scholars equate evil with crime. Finally, theologians deal with evil as sin, and sometimes wrestle with the ultimate origins of evil. Through a sociological lens, social institutions – not individuals – are responsible for "evil." The Hedgehog Review (2000) suggests:

122/ JCJPC 13(2), 2006   Sociologists are unlikely to use the word "evil" in their discussions of social life. But when they do, their focus is often on the social conditions that are conducive to widespread violence and crime. The health of society is at issue in these social problems. The onus for resisting evil is placed on transforming social institutions and conditions, such that the individuals and communities within them will be morally bound to each other in constructive ways. ... Sociological studies make a vital contribution to the study of a subject that has for so long been discussed in abstract terms with no empirical grounding, particularly since the evils that result from corrupt social structures have a much greater capacity for destruction than does a single individual.

Lecter's crimes are merely the consequences of an industrialized European aristocracy that suffered the strains of class stratification, poverty, racism, and that eventually erupted in fascism and war. Like so many other people, Lecter was damaged and scarred by the events of World War II, and has not been able to find solace in the structures that society provides. Lecter's murders are symptomatic of deeper social pathologies (the real evils).

Through a psychological lens, "evil" is a product of mental illness or personality disorders. Viewed from a psychological perspective, though, Lecter is an interesting anomaly. Although he commits acts typically characterized as evil, he is not mentally ill (Oleson, 2005). Although Lecter does not hesitate to torture and kill when he deems it to be appropriate, he does not satisfy the diagnostic criteria for either antisocial personality disorder or sadistic personality disorder. The Hedgehog Review (2000) notes that books on evil written from a psychological perspective tend to take particular forms: interviews with executors of evil, their victims, or those who have had experiences of evil; case studies from clinical practices; meditations on the motivations underlying evil actions; or discussions of how individuals conceive of evil. The strength of this approach is to demonstrate the complexities of evil, to show the reader how varied evil motivations can be, to indicate how destructive a single evil individual can be, and to illustrate how evil replicates itself in its victims. The limitations of the psychological approach, however, include glossing over the structural forces in society that shape moral development and ignoring the role of agency, rationalizing evil by reducing it to pathological biochemistry or a troubled childhood.

Through a legal lens, where evil and crime are synonymous, Lecter is "evil" because he is criminal. His actions – the actus reus of his crimes (homicide and cannibalism) – are condemned by society, but it is Lecter's culpable mental state – his mens rea ("evil mind") that truly designates him as evil. The killing of a human being under some circumstances (e.g., in wartime or during a lawful execution) is non-criminal, but the killing of another human being with malice aforethought is murder, and murder involving the kind of mens rea evident in Lecter's deliberate crimes is first-degree murder – the most culpable (most evil) variety of murder.

Because Lecter's crimes involve the willful and intentional killing of others (and multiple others, at that), he exhibits the most serious kind of evil recognized by the law. Through a theological lens, the concept of evil is related to sin. Instead of attributing evil to flawed biochemistry or the direct consequence of a troubled childhood, the theological approach to evil locates the source of evil within the agent (either in an evil human actor, or in a supernatural force that causes humans to act evilly).

Is evil a person, e.g., Satan, or a force at work in the world and in the wills of humans? Is evil the distortion of good or the lack of a measure of goodness? Is evil a radical choice or a banal thought-less-ness? Is God responsible for evil or are humans? How do humans conceive of evil and how does that relate to their understandings of human nature, the good, and God (Hedgehow Review, 2000)? Two issues about theological evil merit separate consideration. First, the question of whether evil is a merely an absence or a lack of a quality (such as good), or whether it is an affirmative force. Second, the question of whether evil is a fixed and determined quality or whether it is a mutable quality that is neither linked to one's nature (genetics) nor to one's nurture (experiences). Each of these issues will be discussed in turn.

In one of the seminal works on evil, Eichmann in Jerusalem,

Arendt (1964) painted a disturbing portrait of Nazi war criminal Adolf Eichmann, suggesting that evil can emerge from a lack (bland and bureaucratic thoughtlessness) rather than from an affirmative choice. In Arendt's view, diabolical evil can stem from a lack of awareness, empathy, and knowledge. While it may be counterintuitive to think that evil originates from apathy and ignorance, it is also strangely comforting. Far more chilling is the notion that evil might come from knowledge, not ignorance, and that one can be "wise as well as malevolent" (Sexton, 2001). Dery (1999) suggests that the character of Hannibal Lecter "refutes Hannah Arendt's declaration that evil, after Eichmann, is banal and bureaucratic, more a societal or an institutional cancer than a tumor on the soul" (p. 40). Dery argues that Lecter is that tumor. Greenberg (1992) similarly describes him as a "pure study in Coleridgian 'motiveless malignity' … evil so deep and foul it needs no other cause but its own devilish sustenance to thrive upon". Like Milton's (1667/1981) character of Satan, Lecter is a great and terrible villain because he deliberately chooses to defy law and morality. His crimes are born of knowing choice, not ignorance.

The second issue is also perplexing. There are several ways that metaphysical evil could manifest. One way, described above, is for an individual (like Hannibal Lecter) to have an evil essence. Such a person, while not meeting the diagnostic criteria for antisocial personality disorder or clinical sadism, might be "born bad." While it might not be possible to see "evil" in this individual's genetic blueprint, the evil within him would be predictable and determinable. It might even be possible for scientists to measure or identify this kind of evil. More perplexing to criminologists is the possibility that evil is not an inherent quality, but one that depends upon forces that are both non-genetic and non-experiential (e.g., supernatural entities). Metaphysical evil of this kind would not be a fixed quality, but would be caused by unobservable and immeasurable forces. Throughout the world, a number of serious offenders have insisted that evil forces are quite real, and are responsible for terrible crimes. Consider the following examples:

• An intoxicated police inspector in Hiroshima, Japan stole a bag containing 39,000 yen in cash from a bar. When his colleagues asked him if he knew anything about its disappearance, the officer admitted to taking it, explaining his crime by saying that he had been possessed by an evil spirit (Tipsy Cop, 2003).

• In Zimbabwe, a Chivhu policeman raped two of his teenaged daughters, impregnating one. When he was arrested, he claimed that evil spirits had compelled him to commit the crimes (Rapist Cop, 2002).

• In Uganda, a man arrested for attempted suicide claimed that evil spirits had placed the rope around his neck. He said that the spirits had already strangled two of his siblings in this manner (Man Attempts Suicide, 2001).

• A Somali man living in Ireland admitted to killing his son, but claimed that it was like he was in somebody else's body, and insisted that he was merely following the commands of evil spirits (Somalian Claims, 2003).

• In Kobe, Japan, a fifteen-year-old responsible for murdering two primary school students and assaulting three others wrote an essay in which he suggests that evil forces had caused the crimes. The boy wrote, "In any world the same thing repeats itself. What cannot be stopped, cannot be stopped and what cannot be killed, cannot be killed. Sometimes it can be living inside of oneself. It is an evil spirit…. The evil spirit controls me as if it were a skillful puppeteer"

While it may be tempting to discount these crimes as the products of schizophrenia or other forms of mental illness, claims of evil forces are not limited to those foreign jurisdictions where western psychiatry lacks a foothold. Even high-profile offenders who have been deemed sane by psychiatrists have suggested that evil forces may play a role in explaining "inexplicable" crime. Infamous cannibal killer Jeffrey Dahmer told police officers that evil forces may have led him to commit his crimes. Speaking with police officers, Dahmer mused: I have to question whether or not there is an evil force in the world and whether or not I have been influenced by it…. Although I am not sure if there is a God, or if there is a devil, I know that of lately I've been doing a lot of thinking about both, and I have to wonder what has influenced me in my life" (Schwartz, 1992, pp. 200-201).

Beat poet William S. Burroughs claimed to have an answer to Dahmer's questions. In explaining how he had come to shoot his wife, Joan, in the head, Burroughs claimed that an evil force possessed him. He said: Let's see, Joan was sitting in a chair, I was sitting in another chair across the room about six feet away, there was a table, there was a sofa. The gun was in the suitcase and I took it out, and it was loaded, and I was aiming it. I said to Joan, "I guess it's about time for our William Tell act." She took her highball glass and balanced it on top of her head. Why I did it, I don't know, something took over [italics added]. It was an utterly and completely insane thing to do…. I fired one shot, aiming at the glass.

The others in the room, Gene Allerton and Eddie Woods, corroborated Burroughs's account, noting that the gun fired low, hitting Joan in the side of the head, killing her instantly (Morgan, 1988, p. 195-196). But what prompted Burroughs to do the William Tell act in the first place? What prompted him to shoot? Morgan describes the evil force that Burroughs believed was responsible for Joan's death:

The inimical force that had caused him to kill Joan, Burroughs believed quite literally, was an evil spirit that had possessed him. This was a concept more medieval than modern, although whether the evil spirit is seen as coming from within or without, the result is the same. A divided personality with a capacity for wickedness can look for a psychological explanation, or can believe that he is possessed by malignant forces. Both explanations are metaphors for the nature of evil, which religion and the 'ologies' do not satisfactorily define (Morgan, 1988, p. 198).

Morgan makes an important point. Although it may appear unscientific to explain Burroughs' crime as being caused by an evil spirit, neither an evil spirit nor a pathological personality can be empirically measured. Both evil forces and psychopathologies are, at some level, equivalent metaphors. Although neither evil spirits nor personality disorders can be observed or measured directly, new research suggests that it may be possible to operationalize and measure evil.

THE SCIENCE OF EVIL: USING EVIL AS AN EXPLANATION FOR CRIME

"American sociology, after the 1920s, would reject the use of both journalistic and philosophical analyses of evil for a more thoroughly scientific methodology. However, the discipline then was left with great difficulties in discussing evil (now referred to as deviance) without transvaluing it as sickness or as a sign of social malaise or anomie, leaving treatises on the nature of evil to more ethnographically inspired writings such as criminal biographies, novels, plays, and ultimately screenplays."

Of course, most criminologists do not explain crime in terms of evil. Typically, social scientists either ignore the concept of evil or reject it as a legitimate explanation for behavior (Greek, 1992; Hickey, 1991). Simon (2000, p. 24) explains, "Psychiatrists are medically trained and wedded to using the scientific method, so they avoid applying the term 'evil' to the aberrant or horrible acts that they are called upon to understand and explain." Similarly, Dorothy Lewis (a psychiatrist who has interviewed 21 serial killers) has bluntly dismissed evil as "not a scientific concept" (in Leiby,

2002). Some criminology textbooks even introduce the scientific discipline of criminology by contrasting it against an archaic, animistic worldview (i.e., the belief that spiritual forces such as "evil" were responsible for crime) (e.g., Schmalleger, 2002; Siegel, 2003).

Criminologists disagree about what causes crime. Introductory textbooks identify a number of competing theories, ranging from defective biology (Hooton, 1939; Lombroso, 1876) to social learning (Akers, 1998), from rational choice (Clarke & Cornish, 1985; Cornish & Clarke, 1986) to neuropsychological disorder (Raine, 1993; Volkow & Tancredi, 1987) to meta-

But almost all criminologists, as social scientists, agree on at least one fundamental axiom: crime is caused by knowable influences. The etiology of crime can be known. Criminologists, as scientists, believe that events are determined (Hergenhahn, 1997; Society of Natural Science, 2005), and that "for everything that ever happens there are conditions such that, given them, nothing else could happen" (Taylor, 1967, p. 359). Criminologists believe that crime does not simply occur – something causes it – and it is not caused by immeasurable-and-unobservable forces like "evil."

Defying measurement, observation, and even definition, "evil" is an explanation of last resort. Because behavioral scientists, as "soft" scientists, often envy the positivism of "hard" sciences (such as physics and chemistry), they tend to emphasize quantitative methods that produce well-defined and mathematically formulable results (Mizrach, 2005). If it is true that behavioral scientists resort to invoking mental illness only when the offense is so egregious or bizarre that other criminological explanations do not suffice (Samuels, 1975), then ascribing the origins of criminal behavior to something as abstract and ephemeral as "evil" seems even more desperate. Accordingly, criminologists invoke explanations of "evil" only when describing atrocities that elude comprehension: genocide (Arendt, 1964; Staub, 1989), torture (Mohammed, Shaughnessy, Johnson, & Eisenman, 2002), or "motiveless" serial murder (Hickey, 1991; Levin & Fox, 1985) such as that committed by Hannibal Lecter.

Only a handful of social scientists have dared to argue that "evil" is a legitimate subject for scientific inquiry (Diamond, 2003; Goldberg, 1995; Shermer, 2004; Simon, 1996; Watson, 1995).

Most of the research in this direction has generally applied evolutionary theory or made use of abstract psychological concepts. Attempts to link moral evil to concrete and objective measures are rare. Simon (2000, p. 24) has warned that "[e]vil is a thick rope of many complex, twisted, and intertwined strands" and that "[a]n effort to comprehensively define evil is an impossible task, a fool's errand." Psychiatrist Michael Welner (1998), however, has spearheaded an ambitious effort to create an operationalized and validated depravity scale.

Welner has suggested that hitherto "[t]here have been flirtations with psychiatry's ability to define evil, but that's as far as it goes. There's a sense of, 'Can we approach this, because it's so theological?'" (Perina, 2002, p. 16). Through his depravity scale research, Welner seeks to establish empirically-measurable societal standards of what makes a crime depraved (Welner, 2006). He notes: Judges and juries both across the United States and in other countries who decide that a crime is "depraved," "heinous," or "horrible" can assign more severe sentences. Yet there is no standardized definition for such dramatic words that courts already use. And while we may all recognize that some crimes truly separate themselves from others, there is no standard, fair way to distinguish crimes that are the worst of the worst, or "evil" (Welner, 2006, n.p.).

To facilitate meaningful comparison of "evil" actions, Welner has developed a depravity standard instrument, an objective measure based on forensic evidence that distinguishes not who is depraved but rather, what aspects of a given crime are depraved and the degree of a specific crime's depravity. The instrument is being normed through a three-stage process. In the first stage, now completed, professionals from legal and scientific backgrounds issued general guidance. In the second stage, members of the general public are shaping the specific intents, actions, and attitudes that should be included as items of the depravity standard instrument. In the third stage, members of the general public are refining the relative weight of these items (Welner, 2006). If he is successful in developing an instrument to measure depravity, Welner will have made important progress in quantifying and categorizing evil. Although his efforts remain in their infancy, his research may serve as an important starting place in the study of "inexplicable" crime such as serial homicide. Heinous crimes such as those committed by Hannibal Lecter often defy explanation, but an empirical study of evil may eventually allow criminologists to understand the causes of serial murder.

CONCLUSION

"Is Lecter evil, a freakish monster with maroon eyes and a six-fingered hand, or an adult victim of abuse like Gumb and Dolarhyde? Lecter refuses to provide pat answers, unlike the FBI." Simpson, 2000, p. 94 Thomas Harris's quintessential serial killer, Dr. Hannibal Lecter, has been depicted both in print (Harris, 1981, 1988, 1999) and on film (Demme, 1991; Mann, 1986; Ratner, 2002; Scott, 2001), and is a particularly worthwhile figure because he is derived from both real offenders and literary predecessors (Sexton, 2001). Not only is he a compelling paradox (Oleson, 2005), but the character invites us to think about the nature of human evil. Indeed, the public fascination with Hannibal Lecter may have less to do with his shadowy origins as either a vampire-devil (Oleson, 2006) or a victim of acute childhood trauma (Bruno, 2005) than with the challenging questions about heroism and evil that he forces people to confront.

Even within the literary universe of Thomas Harris' Lecter novels, Lecter is a textbook case, studied by FBI agents at Quantico and by psychiatrists in the Baltimore State Hospital for the Criminally Insane (e.g., Harris, 1988, 1999). Why do Harris' fictional FBI agents study this fictional serial killer? They do so because he – like his real-life antecedents Ted Bundy and Ed Kemper – is intelligent and insightful (Egger, 1998; Ressler & Shachtman, 1992). The agents study Lecter because, as a cannibal killer responsible for the ritualized murders of 21 people (Hannibal Lecter, 2005; Harris, 1999), this incredibly gifted serial killer can help them catch other elusive killers. The psychiatrists and the FBI agents in Harris' novels study Lecter like a treasure map. They do not actually hope to cure him: they hope only to use him to capture other quarry. The approach reflects the attitudes of real-life FBI profilers. Heilbroner (1993, p. 147) quotes FBI agent Roy Hazelwood as saying: We're not interested in causes and we're not interested in cures...We're interested in identification, apprehension, incarceration and prosecution. I'm interested in what I can learn from them or from their wives or girlfriends that can help me more quickly identify them. Let somebody else figure out why.

Criminologists are those other somebodies. By asking why Hannibal Lecter commits his crimes, criminologists may be able to use the Lecter novels and movies as a catalyst for the study of the etiology of serial homicide. The character of Hannibal Lecter is, after all, based on real-life serial killers, and provides readers and viewers with an intimate (if hyperbolic) case study of an organized serial killer. Characters drawn from novels can serve as valuable heuristic devices (Campbell, 1988), teaching us a great deal about the nature of crime and evil. Well-executed depictions of film villains also can teach us a great deal about these things: Film provides an opportunity for dialogue; in that sense, it has always been an interactive medium. If David Lynch or Martin Scorsese displays the human face of evil in Frank or Max Cady, that is only half of the conversation. The other half is ours. It's our responsibility to mull over our feelings about these characters, understand them (or not) and, in the process, define our own moral boundaries (Hinson, 1993).

In addition to teaching viewers something about their own morality, the film character of Hannibal Lecter can teach social scientists a great deal about how serial killers are depicted in popular culture (Jenkins, 1994; Simpson, 2000). Dery (1999, p. 40) promises, "Hannibal Lecter ... offers a skeleton key for unlocking the true nature of our age of tabloid frenzies and talk-show pathologies, serial killers and the women who love them." In many ways, the character of Hannibal Lecter is like a Rorschach blot. The viewer who looks for a textbook organized serial killer in Lecter will find it in him (Oleson, 2005), but so shall the viewer who looks for a criminal genius (Oleson, 2005), a devil or a vampire (Oleson, 2006), or a heroic victim of childhood trauma. Hannibal Lecter dwells at the intersection of these contradictions, and is attractive because he is both man and monster, devil and avenging angel, villain and victim. The public's fascination with Hannibal Lecter says as much about the public as it does about Lecter. Ultimately, careful study of Hannibal Lecter might teach criminologists something more about the kind of a society that produces such killers and about the kind of society that remains obsessed by them (Oleson, 2005).

Joseph Paul Franklin

White Supremacist Joseph Franklin

It was a deadly mix: a mentally troubled man from an abusive, broken home turned radical racist and then serial killer.

His name was Joseph Paul Franklin, and he went on a horrific killing spree beginning in 1977 at the age of 27. Before his reign of murder ended in 1980, he took the lives of at least 15 men, women, and children in some 11 states. He also admitted shooting civil rights leader Vernon Jordan and paralyzing pornography publisher Larry Flynt.

Franklin—born James Clayton Vaughn, Jr. before changing his name to reflect his admiration for Benjamin Franklin and Nazi Joseph Goebbels—was drawn to white supremacist ideologies as a teen. Dropping out of high school following a severe eye injury, he got married, became an abusive husband, and began racking up minor legal violations.

As his association with white supremacist groups grew, Franklin became increasingly confrontational toward minorities. By the mid-1970s, he had rejected even the most radical hate groups because he didn't think they took their hatred far enough. He wanted to attack, not just sit around complaining. His self-directed "mission," he later suggested, was to incite his fellow supremacists to action.

The summer of 1976 marked a turning point. On Labor Day weekend in Atlanta, Franklin followed an interracial couple and sprayed them with mace. This was his first known physical attack...it escalated from there. On July 29, 1977, he bombed a Tennessee synagogue; a few days later in Wisconsin, he killed two men—one black and one white—after encountering them in a parking lot.

For the next three years, Franklin drifted across the country, robbing banks (with some proficiency, according to law enforcement investigators) and using a sniper rifle to target his victims. He killed possibly more than 20 people and seriously injured six more.

By 1980, the FBI and its partners were closing in on Franklin. The often vast miles and lack of evidentiary connections between his crimes—as well as his skill at living the life of an anonymous drifter—kept Franklin under the radar for a time. This changed in September 1980, when an observant police officer in Kentucky noticed a gun in the back of a car Franklin was driving. A records check showed an outstanding warrant, and Franklin was brought in for questioning. He escaped while being detained, but the Bureau was on his trail.

Evidence from the car suggested multiple connections to the racially motivated sniper attacks across the country. The Bureau's behavioral analysts contributed their insights, and the FBI shared its growing knowledge of Franklin's characteristics and tactics with law enforcement and the public. Two details were crucial—Franklin's racist tattoos and his reliance on blood bank donations for cash while between bank robberies.

Within weeks, a blood-bank operator in Florida contacted the Bureau about a man matching Franklin's description. FBI agents immediately tracked him to Lakeland, Florida and arrested him on October 28, 1980.

Franklin faced legal action across the U.S. for the next two decades, eventually being convicted of multiple murders, attacks, and other crimes at both the state and federal levels. He was sentenced to life in prison and received the death penalty in several states. On November 11, 2013, he was executed in Missouri for the 1977 murder of a man standing in front of a synagogue in St. Louis.

The FBI's Role Takes Shape

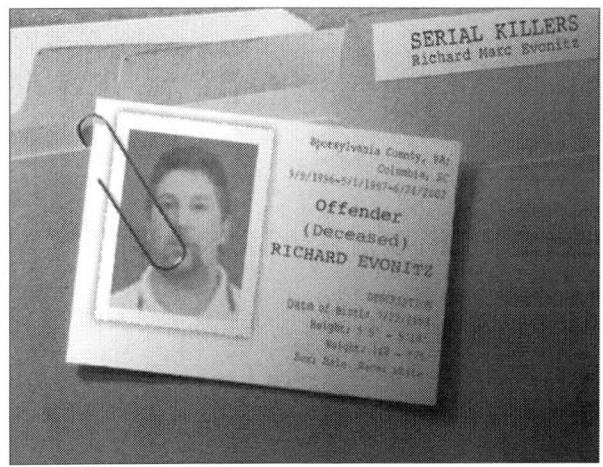

Richard Marc Evonitz committed three murders in Virginia. Over the years, the FBI has played a slowly evolving role in addressing the threat of serial killers.

Seventeen years ago yesterday—on September 9, 1996—a teenager disappeared from her home in Spotsylvania County, Virginia. Tragically, she was found dead the following month. The next May, two sisters in the same county went missing after coming home from school. Five days later, their bodies were found in a river about 40 miles away.

This trio of murders was the work of a serial killer named Richard Marc Evonitz. It took another five years for him to be identified. In June 2002, after a teenage girl managed to escape from a kidnapper in South Carolina, she identified Evonitz as her abductor. He fled to Florida and committed suicide as authorities closed in. Valuable trace evidence collected by the FBI later definitively linked him to the murders of the three Virginia girls. He is suspected of more homicides and other attacks.

Although relatively rare, serial killings have both horrified and fascinated the American people for decades. Serial murderers (see sidebar for the FBI's definition) have existed throughout history and have been popularized by such killers as Jack the Ripper in England and Herman Webster Mudgett in the United States in the late 1800s. The exact origin of the term serial killer or serial murderer is not known, but it appears to have come into use in law enforcement circles in the 1970s and more commonly in society in the 1980s and 1990s.

Over the years, the FBI has played a slowly evolving role in addressing the threat of serial killers. In its earliest days, few violent crimes fell under the Bureau's jurisdiction. It depended on where the crime occurred—if it was on government property, the high seas, or certain Indian reservations, the FBI took charge. In the 1930s, the FBI became a household name as it tackled violent gangsters and gained more law enforcement authorities in the process. In the 1950s and '60s, the Bureau supported local and state law enforcement in some high-profile serial killer cases like the Boston Strangler and the Zodiac Killer of Northern California.

It was in the 1970s, however, that the FBI's role in addressing serial killers began to grow as new capabilities were developed. Building on earlier work in New York and elsewhere, Special Agent Howard Teten and others in the Bureau began to apply the insights of psychology and behavioral science to violent criminal behavior in a comprehensive way. Since then, the FBI has become a leader in behavioral analysis, providing an array of support and training to help identify serial killers and to prevent future violence.

The FBI's involvement in serial killer cases has also evolved under federal law. For example, the Bureau was authorized to investigate violent crimes against interstate travelers in 1994 and serial killings specifically in 1998. The FBI may investigate only when requested to do so by an appropriate law enforcement agency. The Bureau is also authorized to provide a variety of support services, from laboratory and behavioral analysis to crime statistics collection and the sharing of criminal identification and history information through our longstanding services and systems.

In the coming months, FBI.gov will examine the Bureau's role in addressing serial killings in more detail, including our work in some of the most horrific serial murder investigations in the last 40 years.

The Birth of Behavioral Analysis in the FBI

Behavioral analysis seeks to understand the behavior, experiences, and psychological make-up of criminals and suspects for insights that could solve cases. It played a role in the case of serial killer Ted Bundy.

In the final days of 1977, a man now known as one of the most prolific serial killers in U.S. history—Theodore "Ted" Bundy—cleverly escaped from a Colorado prison while most of the staff was away for the holidays.

FBI agents quickly joined the search. In early February 1978, the Bureau placed Bundy on its Ten Most Wanted Fugitives list. Among the information shared by the FBI with law enforcement during this time were details on his "M.O." (modus operandi or method of operation). Bundy typically looked for victims at places where young people gathered, such as colleges, beaches, ski resorts, and discos, the FBI explained. And he preferred young, attractive women with long hair parted in the middle.

The synopsis was pulled from a psychological assessment of Ted Bundy prepared by two FBI agents—Howard Teten and Robert Ressler—at the Bureau's Training Academy. The two men were part of a groundbreaking behavioral analysis unit set up five years earlier for precisely this purpose: to study the behavior, experiences, and psychological make-up of criminals and suspects for patterns and insights that could help solve cases and prevent future crimes, especial serial murders and other forms of violence.

Criminal behavioral analysis wasn't a new concept. In the 1940s and 1950s, for example, George Metsky—the so-called "Mad Bomber"—planted explosive devices around New York City until a behavioral profile developed for the police by a local criminologist and psychiatrist helped lead to his capture in 1957. But in the coming years, the FBI would take this innovation to a whole new level.

At the center of this evolution was Teten. He had joined the FBI as an agent in 1962, already with an interest in the psychological aspects of criminal behavior (see sidebar). In 1969, he was recruited by the

Training Division to be an instructor, and around 1970, he convinced his supervisor to let him teach a workshop in "applied criminology." His first course was a four-hour lecture to New York police; it was a hit. Next, he gave the course at a regional police training school in Texas, expanding it to four days. By about day three, students were bringing up unsolved cases. Based on insights from a class discussion, one student interviewed a suspect—and the man confessed.

Word spread, and interest in the course skyrocketed. So Teten borrowed FBI New York Special Agent Patrick Mullany, who had a master's degree in educational psychology, and the two began teaching together. Teten would outline the facts of a case, and Mullany would show how aspects of the criminal's personality were revealed in the crime scene. According to Teten, "Patrick really made a difference, because he was a fully qualified psychologist, where I was a criminologist." Soon Mullany was reassigned to Quantico permanently.

In 1972, the FBI stood up a behavioral science unit to advance the concepts the pair was teaching throughout the FBI and across law enforcement; it was led by Supervisory Special Agent Jack Kirsch and included Teten and Mullany (Ressler joined in 1975)—and their growing education, research, and service responsibilities. As the unit developed, so did the FBI's study and understanding of serial killers.

And Ted Bundy? Five days after landing on the FBI's Top Ten list, he was caught by a Florida policeman. He was ultimately convicted of multiple murders and executed in 1989.

A Founding Father of Behavioral Analysis

Howard Teten's fascination with criminal psychology started early in his law enforcement career. A Marine Corps sergeant and photographer during the Korean War, he took a job with the Orange County (California) Sheriff's Department in 1956. His budding interests in photography and criminal investigations quickly brought him into contact with the area crime lab, which encouraged him to pursue the study of criminology. Taking a position as a police officer in San Leandro in 1958, Teten began studying criminology at the University of California and earned a degree in 1960.

It was at Berkeley that the psychological aspects of criminal behavior caught Teten's attention. "Here I am at school, taking courses in abnormal psychology, criminal psychology—and [also] working crime scenes on a daily basis," he later recalled, "and I'm beginning to see parallels."

Teten accepted an appointment with the FBI because it offered better advancement opportunities for the young family man. He entered new agent training in April 1962 and was assigned to the Oklahoma City Field Office. He was transferred to Cincinnati in 1963 and Memphis in 1965. There, he ran the office's police training program and worked on his master's degree in social psychology at Memphis State University. He gained the attention of the FBI's Training Division and took a job as an instructor in Washington, D.C. in July 1969. The rest, as they say, is history.

Ted Bundy's Campaign of Terror

A $100,000 reward was offered for Ted Bundy's capture.

No one knows when or where Theodore "Ted" Bundy killed for the first time. It could have been during his teenage years or when he was in his early 20s in the late 1960s. It might have been in Washington state, where he resided for many years, or on the East Coast, where he was born and lived as a young boy and had family ties.

But we do know that by 1974, Ted Bundy's prolific reign of terror and murder was underway. In Washington state, young, attractive female college students began disappearing. Local police investigated, and clues began to emerge. Witnesses pointed to a Volkswagen Beetle and a young man on crutches or with an arm in a sling.

Bundy moved to Salt Lake City that summer, and the murders continued in Utah, Idaho, and Colorado. In August 1975, police arrested Bundy for the first time after pulling him over in his Volkswagen and finding suspicious items—including handcuffs, rope, and a ski mask—that investigators later linked to missing women. In February of the following year, he was found guilty of kidnapping and assaulting a Utah teenager who had managed to escape from him, landing in prison for up to 15 years.

Meanwhile, investigators from multiple states were piecing together the string of murders. In 1976, Bundy was charged with killing a vacationing nursing student, and he found himself in Aspen, Colorado in June 1977 for a preliminary hearing. Left alone at one point, Bundy let himself out of a second story window, jogged down Main Street, and disappeared. Extensive searches were made, and the FBI quickly began to gather and disseminate Bundy's criminal history and identification information. Soon after, FBI agents swore out a federal arrest warrant for unlawful flight to avoid confinement, and a $100,000 reward was offered for his capture.

Bundy didn't make it far; he was located in Aspen a few days later. But he bided his time and seized another opportunity for escape on New Year's Eve in 1977—slipping through an opening in the ceiling of his cell and sneaking out through the jailer's office.

A nationwide manhunt followed, and the FBI played a central role. We created a series of wanted posters and other identification material, processed latent fingerprints from around the country, provided insight from our Behavioral Analysis Unit, and—as the days stretched into weeks—added Bundy to our Ten Most Wanted Fugitives list on February 10, 1978.

Tragically, Bundy continued his murder spree while on the run. On the evening of January 14, he invaded a Florida State University sorority house, brutally killing two co-eds and leaving a third with serious injuries.

But the net was closing. Around 1:30 a.m. on February 15, a Pensacola police officer noticed a stolen orange Volkswagen Beetle driving west on Cervantes Street and ordered the car to pull over. Bundy resisted but was eventually taken into custody.

The officer had no idea who was inside the car, but Bundy was quickly identified with the help of the FBI's fugitive flyer and was soon back in Colorado to face murder charges. He was eventually convicted and executed, but not before admitting to more than two dozen murders over many years. There may have been even more. To this day, Ted Bundy remains one of the nation's most deadly and notorious serial killers.

WANTED BY THE FBI
INTERSTATE FLIGHT - MURDER

THEODORE ROBERT BUNDY
DESCRIPTION

Born November 24, 1946, Burlington, Vermont (not supported by birth records); Height, 5'11" to 6'; Weight, 145 to 175 pounds; Build, slender, athletic; Hair, dark brown, collar length; Eyes, blue; Complexion, pale / sallow; Race, white; Nationality, American; Occupations, bellboy, busboy, cook's helper, dishwasher, janitor, law school student, office worker, political campaign worker, psychiatric social worker, salesman, security guard; Scars and Marks, mole on neck, scar on scalp; Social Security Number used, 533-44-4655; Remarks, occasionally stammers when upset; has worn glasses, false mustache and beard as disguise in past; left-handed; can imitate British accent; reportedly physical fitness and health enthusiast.

CRIMINAL RECORD
Bundy has been convicted of aggravated kidnaping.

CAUTION
BUNDY, A COLLEGE-EDUCATED PHYSICAL FITNESS ENTHUSIAST WITH A PRIOR HISTORY OF ESCAPE, IS BEING SOUGHT AS A PRISON ESCAPEE AFTER BEING CONVICTED OF KIDNAPING AND WHILE AWAITING TRIAL INVOLVING A BRUTAL SEX SLAYING OF A WOMAN AT A SKI RESORT. HE SHOULD BE CONSIDERED ARMED, DANGEROUS AND AN ESCAPE RISK.

FBI/DOJ

Wayne Williams and the Atlanta Child Murders

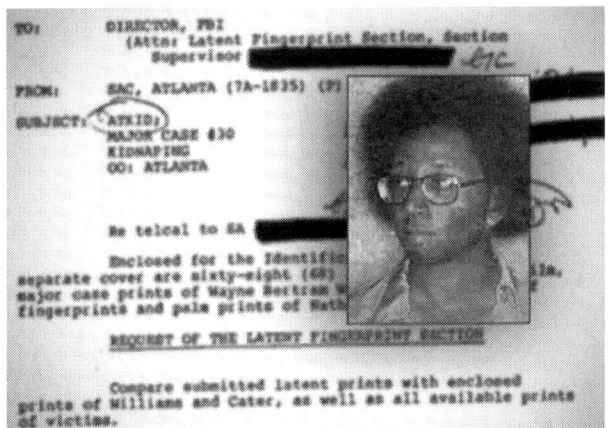

Evidence linked Wayne Williams, inset above over one of the files in his case, to 22 murders in Atlanta beginning in 1979. The FBI's involvement began in 1980 following the abduction of a 7-year-old girl.

On July 21, 1979, a 14-year-old boy disappeared. Four days later, another teen went missing. Both, it was soon learned, had been killed.

It was the beginning of a shocking series of murders—some 29 in all—that would take place over the next 22 months in Atlanta. The victims were all young African-Americans, and as the death toll mounted, so did fear and tension across the city.

The FBI's involvement in the case began on June 22, 1980 following the abduction of a 7-year-old girl. The Atlanta Police Department, which—along with the Georgia Bureau of Investigation—was investigating the string of killings, asked the FBI if the federal kidnapping statute had been violated.

None of the crimes appeared to fall under federal law, but Special Agent in Charge John Glover—the first African-American to lead an FBI field office—offered all the support the Bureau could give under the circumstances. Our Atlanta office helped follow up on out-of-state leads. The FBI Lab provided assistance. And our Behavioral Sciences Unit sent an expert to develop a profile of a possible perpetrator.

Meanwhile, the murders continued. Local politicians, the news media, and even Georgia Senator Sam Nunn asked the Department of Justice to permit FBI involvement, and the attorney general did so on November 6, 1980, authorizing a preliminary investigation. On November 17, the Bureau launched a major case investigation, devoting more than two dozen agents and other personnel to the case full time.

FBI agents joined local and state law enforcement officers on a task force investigating the murders. Collectively, they focused on a dozen disappearances with several shared traits. The victims were all young African-American males who vanished in broad daylight in fairly public locations. Their bodies were found in desolate areas. Their murders had no obvious motivation (in contrast, two other homicides from that period appeared to have been gang-related). These commonalities suggested a single killer.

The City of Atlanta formally asked for FBI assistance on

CITY OF ATLANTA

LEE P. BROWN
PUBLIC SAFETY COMMISSIONER

August 21, 1980

Mr. John Glover
Special Agent in Charge
Federal Bureau of Investigation
275 Peachtree Street, Room 925
Atlanta, Georgia 30303

Dear Mr. Glover:

Within the last six months, the city of Atlanta has experienced a dramatic increase in the number of homicides and missing person reports involving children under the age of 15. To date, we have six unsolved homicides and four missing person reports with foul play suspected. To address this problem, the Bureau of Police Services has formed a special task force to investigate these crimes, but we have a limitation on our resources.

Your previous assistance in this matter has been greatly appreciated and should prove very helpful as we proceed in investigating these cases. However, the scope of the problem and the extreme sensitivity in which these cases must be investigated compel me to request your further assistance. Specifically, I am hereby requesting that you assign two agents on a full time basis to assist our task force. I make this request with the full understanding that the cases do not necessarily fall under the jurisdiction of the federal government. We do need, nevertheless, the professional expertise that can be provided to us from your agency in the form of technical assistance and support.

Chief of Police George Napper will be available to discuss this request with you in greater detail. I do, however, hope that you will be able to honor our request and sincerely appreciate your efforts toward that end.

7-1835-5

Yours for a safer Atlanta,

Lee P. Brown

XC 80-633 (APD)

50

The case continued through the winter and into the spring of 1981. By late April, however, the killer began to change his behavior, dumping the victims' bodies in the Chattahoochee River. Members of the task force staked out the 14 bridges in the Atlanta metropolitan area that crossed the river and patiently waited.

On May 22, a big break came in the case. One of the groups conducting surveillance—consisting of an FBI agent, an Atlanta police officer, and two police cadets—heard a loud splash around 2:52 a.m. A car sped across the bridge, turned around in a parking lot on the other side, and sped back across the bridge. The vehicle was pursued and stopped. The driver was a 23-year-old African-American freelance photographer named Wayne Williams.

Lacking probable cause, authorities let Williams go. But when the body of a young African-American man named Nathaniel Cater was found downstream two days later, more attention was paid to Williams. Investigators soon learned that his alibi was poor and that he had been arrested earlier that year for impersonating a police officer. Later, he failed multiple polygraph examinations.

Williams was arrested on June 21, 1981. He was convicted of two murders on February 27, 1982, after he was linked to the victims through meticulous hair and fiber analysis and witness testimony.

51

Following the trial, the law enforcement task force concluded that there was enough evidence to link Williams to another 20 of the 29 deaths. He went to jail for life, and the Atlanta child killings stopped.

Andrew Cunanan Murders a Fashion Icon

Murderer Andrew Cunanan was added to the FBI's Ten Most Wanted Fugitives list on June 12, 1997, shortly before he killed Gianni Versace.

Around 8:45 on the morning of July 15, 1997, international fashion designer Gianni Versace returned home to his Miami Beach mansion on Ocean Drive following a walk to a local café.

Suddenly, a man approached Versace, pulled out a pistol, and killed him with two shots to the back of his head. The man fled— followed at a distance by at least one witness—and disappeared into a nearby parking garage.

Miami Beach homicide detectives soon asked for assistance from the FBI's local field office in the city. The officers were concerned that the killing might be a murder-for-hire, but evidence quickly suggested that it wasn't. Inside the parking garage identified by the witness was a red pickup truck linked to a murder in New Jersey and a man named Andrew Phillip Cunanan, the target of an ongoing manhunt.

Cunanan was a 27-year-old college dropout from California. He was highly intelligent, spoke two languages, and since his teenage years had sought to live a life of riches and comfort. He had supplemented his earnings from an odd job here and there by serving as a male prostitute and engaging in longer-term liaisons with older homosexuals who would shower him with gifts and cash.

For reasons that remain unclear, Cunanan had begun a murderous spree in late April 1997. First, he bludgeoned a former naval officer to death with a hammer in Minneapolis. A few days later, he shot and killed an architect and dumped his body near East Rush Lake in Minnesota. Both men were his long-time associates. In May, Cunanan targeted a stranger—a 72-year-old real estate developer—in Chicago. Cunanan stole the man's car, and, less than a week later, murdered a cemetery worker in New Jersey. He then took that victim's red truck and drove to Miami.

Throughout this time, authorities were putting together the pieces. The investigation and forensic work linked the Chicago murder and the others to Cunanan. On May 7, the FBI joined the search for Cunanan and quickly marshaled its resources to identify and interview his friends, family, and other contacts. The New Jersey murder made it clear Cunanan was moving across the country, and gay groups were especially concerned that he might insinuate himself into their circles and continue to commit murders. The New York City Gay and Lesbian Anti-Violence Project posted a large reward and sought to warn those who might know Cunanan.

Working with the television show America's Most Wanted, the FBI made Cunanan the 449th addition to its Ten Most Wanted Fugitives list on June 12, 1997. Our offices in Minnesota, California, Illinois, New Jersey, and elsewhere continued to seek information about him. The Bureau also publicized a telephone tip line and disseminated details on the FBI's public website. But Cunanan slipped under the radar.

With the murder of Gianni Versace, though, the net began to close. Eight days later, on July 23, 1997, the caretaker of a houseboat about two miles north of Versace's house in Miami

Beach reported hearing a gunshot. Responders found Cunanan dead from a self-inflicted wound. His killing spree was over.

The FBI and Jeffrey Dahmer

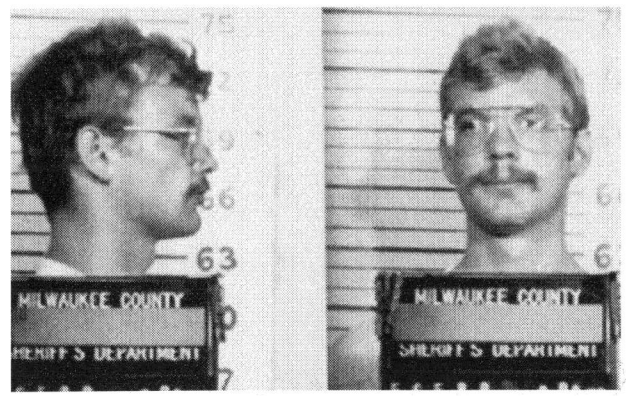

In this 1991 handout from the Milwaukee County Sheriff's Department, serial killer Jeffrey Dahmer is seen in a police mugshot. (AP Photo/Milwaukee County Sheriff's Department)

At about 11:30 on the night of July 22, 1991, Milwaukee Police Department patrol units saw a partially clothed man stumbling down the road near an apartment building on North 25th Street. A handcuff could be seen dangling from his wrist. The young man reported to police that he had been threatened with a knife inside that apartment building, prompting the officers to investigate. And the first report on the incident to FBI Headquarters indicated that the police arrested a man named Jeffrey Dahmer at his apartment, where they had discovered what could have been the set of a horror movie—numerous body parts belonging to multiple victims.

In serial murder cases, the FBI's role is often that of providing forensic and other investigative support in an ongoing investigation. That was certainly the case with Dahmer.

After analyzing our options regarding jurisdiction in this case under the federal kidnapping statute, the Bureau offered its laboratory and identification services to local authorities in Milwaukee. To help identify previous victims, investigators began tracing the killer's trail across the U.S. and around the world. Behavioral analysts, also known as profilers, participated as well.

The remains of 11 victims were found in Dahmer's apartment. Evidence recovered there—from physical remains to tools used to torture and dismember victims—was sent to FBI Headquarters for forensic analysis. The Bureau ran DNA profiles; conducted chemical, biological, and tool mark analyses; undertook photographic and computer examinations; and performed other tests on submitted evidence. Bureau agents and analysts also investigated whether Dahmer could be linked to unsolved murders in areas where he was known to have lived, including Ohio, Florida, and Germany—one of the locations Dahmer was stationed while in the U.S. Army.

Soon after his arrest, Dahmer confessed to committing more than a dozen murders that included the torture and mutilation of his victims and the abuse of their corpses.

In early 1992, Wisconsin prosecutors—armed with evidence provided by the Bureau— began to set forth charges that Dahmer had killed 15 men during the course of a long criminal career. He was sentenced to life in prison and extradited to Ohio, where he was convicted of another murder. In 1994, while serving his sentence in a Wisconsin prison, Dahmer was bludgeoned to death by a fellow inmate.

The FBI's involvement in serial killer cases has evolved over time. In the 1970s, we began applying the insights of psychology and behavioral science to violent criminal behavior. Federal legislation on serial killings in 1988 and on violent crimes against interstate travelers in 1994 expanded our operational jurisdiction. And of course, advancements in forensics over the years—such as DNA analysis and automated fingerprint capabilities—have played, and will continue to play, a vital role in stopping these killers and identifying their victims.

More about the FBI's role in this case can be found on the FBI Vault, where we have made our Freedom of Information Act release of material on Dahmer available. This material was released a number of years ago and includes our Headquarters file, Milwaukee Division file, a file from the FBI Laboratory concerning tests made on evidence from Dahmer's apartment, and a foreign police cooperation file on efforts to determine if Dahmer had killed anyone while living in Germany.

Mad Bomber George Metesky

How New York's Mad Bomber George Metesky was brought down by pioneer profiler

It took 16 years but the first bomb set by George Metesky, 75 years ago today, shaped crime's first psychological profile which quickly led to the arrest of New York's Mad Bomber.

Metesky's terror campaign began when Consolidated Edison energy company workers on West 64th Street in Manhattan found a homemade pipe bomb on a windowsill on November 16, 1940.

Attached was a note in block-style handwriting saying: "Con

Edison crooks, this is for you."

The small, crudely made pipe bomb did not explode and police believed the note's placement indicated it was never intended to detonate. Police investigated disgruntled employees and other possible suspects, then dropped the case.

A second unexploded bomb was found in September, 1941, on 19th St, a few blocks from Consolidated Edison's Irving Plaza offices. The bomb, found in an old sock, had a similar to construction to the November, 1940, bomb, but no note.

In December, shortly after the Japanese attack on Pearl Harbor, another letter, signed F.P. and written in block-style handwriting, arrived at New York police headquarters. It explained the bomber would desist for the duration of WWII, adding, "Later I will bring the Con Edison to justice. They will pay for their dastardly deeds."

New York Mad Bomber George Metesky, in his buttoned-up suit,

is taken into custody.

The next bomb was found on March 29, 1950, at Grand Central Station. In April a bomb exploded in a phone booth inside New York Public Library, followed by another at Grand Central Station. Over the next five years, nearly 30 bombs made of pipe, black powder and watch components were planted at New York's Port Authority Bus Terminal, Radio City Music Hall, in movie theatres and phone booths, and Penn Station where an elderly men's-room attendant was seriously injured when a bomb exploded in a toilet bowl in February, 1956.

Nearly half the bombs exploded, causing more than a dozen injuries but no deaths.

An explosion just before 8pm on Sunday, December 2, 1956, at Brooklyn Paramount Theatre during a screening of War And Peace infuriated frustrated detectives. Planted at the back of the orchestra section, flying metal injured three patrons.

Detectives recognised the workmanship of the phantom they called the Mad Bomber. In desperation, New York Police Department Crime Laboratory Inspector Howard Finney and police captain John Cronin approached Cronin's friend James Brussel, a criminologist, psychiatrist and assistant commissioner at New York State Commission for Mental Hygiene.

After studying crime scene photos and notes from FP, Brussel drew up a detailed description of the suspect. He predicted the bomber was unmarried, foreign-born, self-educated, in his 50s, lived in Connecticut and was paranoid, with a vendetta against Con Edison.

Although some of Brussel's predictions were common sense, others such as the bomber's age drew on psychological study. Bussel noted paranoia tended to peak around age 35, so 16 years after setting the first bomb put the bomber in his 50s.

Ciminologist Dr. James A Brussel, whose profile of the Mad Bomber, helped police get their man. Image: Corbis

The New York Times published Bussel's profile on December 25, 1956, although it did not mention the bomber was likely of Slavic origin, and would be wearing a double-breasted suit, buttoned up.

The profile and a newspaper promise to achieve justice for the bomber induced him to send letters. On January 19, 1957, FP sent a letter explaining he developed pneumonia and later tuberculosis after laying unnoticed for hours on "cold concrete" following an accident at Con Edison.

The letter detailed his lost compensation case and the "perjury" of co-workers about events of September 5, 1931.

Con Edison clerk Alice Kelly had been scouring company workers' compensation files for "troublesome" case files where threats were made or implied. On January 18, 1957, she found a file marked in red with the words "injustice" and "permanent disability", as written in the bomber's newspaper letters.

The file identified George Metesky, an employee injured after inhaling scalding boiler fumes in a plant accident on September 5, 1931. Disabled for 26 weeks, he was terminated by Edison then had compensation claims dismissed because he waited too long.

When police knocked on the door of a house in Waterbury, Connecticut, at 11pm on January 21, 1957, a smiling middle-aged man wearing pyjamas answered.

"I know why you fellows are here," he told police.

"You think I'm the Mad Bomber."

Asked to get dressed, Metesky returned with his hair neatly combed, his shoes newly shined and wearing a double-breasted suit — buttoned.

Metesky confessed but was declared a paranoid schizophrenic after psychiatric evaluations. Incompetent to stand trial, Metesky was committed to a New York hospital for the criminally insane.

Released in December 1973, he died at home in 1994.

George "Machine Gun" Kelly

At 11:15 p.m., on Saturday, July 22, 1933, Mr. and Mrs. Charles F. Urschel, one of Oklahoma's wealthiest couples, were playing bridge with their friends, Mr. and Mrs. Walter R. Jarrett, on a screened porch of the Urschel residence at Oklahoma City. Two men, one armed with a machine gun and the other with a pistol, opened the screen door and inquired which of the two men was Mr. Urschel. Receiving no reply, they remarked, "Well, we will take both of them." After warning the women against calling for help, they marched Urschel and Jarrett to where they had driven their car, put them into the back of the Chevrolet sedan, and drove rapidly away.

Mrs. Urschel, in accordance with the attorney general's advice to the public, immediately telephoned J. Edgar Hoover, Director of the FBI. Special agents were sent to Oklahoma City, where an extensive investigation commenced.

At 1:00 a.m., Sunday, July 23, 1933, Jarrett made his way back to the Urschel residence. The victims had been driven to the outskirts of the city, where they had turned right on a dirt road parallel to the 23rd Street Highway and had proceeded northeast to a point about twelve miles from the city. After crossing a small bridge and arriving at an intersection, they had put Jarrett out of the car after they had identified him and had taken $50 which he had in his wallet, warning him not to tell the direction the kidnappers had gone. He stated that after he was released the car proceeded south.

After the kidnapping became known, numerous letters, telephone calls, and other leads were received, many of which were anonymous, indicating possible leads. All had to be followed, although few were of value. Leads of this nature were developed simultaneously in all parts of the United States.

Several days elapsed before word was received from the kidnappers. On July 26, J.G. Catlett, a wealthy oil man of Tulsa, Oklahoma and an intimate friend of Mr. Urschel, received a package through Western Union. It contained a letter written to him by Mr. Urschel, requesting Mr. Catlett to act as an intermediary for his release; a personal letter from Mr. Urschel to his wife; and a typewritten note directed to Mr. Catlett, demanding that he proceed to Oklahoma City immediately and not communicate by telephone or otherwise with the Urschel family from Tulsa. The package also contained a typewritten letter addressed to Mr. E. E. Kirkpatrick of Oklahoma City, which read in part.

"Immediately upon receipt of this letter you will proceed to obtain the sum of TWO HUNDRED THOUSAND DOLLARS ($200,000.00) in GENUINE USED FEDERAL RESERVE CURRENCY in the denomination of TWENTY DOLLARS ($20.00) Bills.

It will be useless for you to attempt taking notes of SERIAL NUMBERS MAKING UP DUMMY PACKAGE, OR ANYTHING ELSE IN THE LINE OF ATTEMPTED DOUBLE CROSS. BEAR THIS IN MIND, CHARLES F. URSCHEL WILL REMAIN IN OUR CUSTODY UNTIL MONEY HAS BEEN INSPECTED AND EXCHANGED AND FURTHERMORE WILL BE AT THE SCENE OF CONTACT FOR PAY-OFF AND IF THERE SHOULD BE ANY ATTEMPT AT ANY DOUBLE XX IT WILL BE HE THAT SUFFERS THE CONSEQUENCE.

RUN THIS AD FOR ONE WEEK IN DAILY OKLAHOMAN.

'FOR SALE — 160 Acres Land, good five room house, deep well. Also Cows, Tools, Tractor, Corn, and Hay. $3750.00 for quick sale. . TERMS. . Box # _____'

You will hear from us as soon as convenient after insertion of AD."

The ad was inserted.

On July 28, an envelope addressed to the "Daily Oklahoman," Box H-807, was received. It was from Joplin, Missouri. A letter to Kirkpatrick read in part:

" . . . You will pack TWO HUNDRED THOUSAND DOLLARS ($200,000.00) in USED GENUINE FEDERAL RESERVE NOTES OF TWENTY DOLLAR DENOMINATION in a suitable LIGHT COLORED LEATHER BAG and have someone purchase transportation for you, including berth, aboard Train #28 (The Sooner) which departs at 10:10 p.m. via the M. K. & T. Lines for Kansas City, Mo.

You will ride on the OBSERVATION PLATFORM where you may be observed by some-one at some Station along the Line between Okla. City and K. C. Mo. If indication are alright, somewhere along the Right-of-Way you will observe a Fire on the

Right Side of Track (Facing direction train is bound) that first Fire will be your Cue to be prepared to throw BAG to Track immediately after passing SECOND FIRE.

REMEMBER THIS — IF ANY TRICKERY IS ATTEMPTED YOU WILL FIND THE REMAINS OF URSCHEL AND INSTEAD OF JOY THERE WILL BE DOUBLE GRIEF — FOR, SOME-ONE VERY NEAR AND DEAR TO THE URSCHEL FAMILY IS UNDER CONSTANT SURVEILLANCE AND WILL LIKE-WISE SUFFER FOR YOUR ERROR.

"If there is the slightest HITCH in these PLANS for any reason what-so-ever, not your fault, you will proceed on into Kansas City, Mo. and register at the Muehlebach Hotel under the name of E. E. Kincaid of Little Rock, Arkansas and await further instructions there.

THE MAIN THING IS DO NOT DIVULGE THE CONTENTS OF THIS LETTER TO ANY LAW AUTHORITIES FOR WE HAVE NO INTENTION OF FURTHER COMMUNICATION.

YOU ARE TO MAKE THIS TRIP SATURDAY JULY 29TH 1933 . . . "

The Bureau's first concern in all kidnapping cases is the safe return of the kidnapped victim. Accordingly, no effort was made on the part of the Bureau to identify the writer of these letters or to interfere in any way with the negotiations until after Urschel was returned.

As a result of the above letters, $200,000 in used $20 notes of the Federal Reserve Bank, Tenth District, was obtained and the serial numbers recorded. They were placed in a new, light-colored leather Gladstone bag. At the same time, another identical bag was purchased and filled with old magazines, fearing an attempt at hijacking. As a precaution, it was decided that Catlett would accompany Kirkpatrick to Kansas City. By prearrangement, Catlett sat just inside the rear end of the observation car, while Kirkpatrick sat on the observation platform with the bag containing the magazines. Kirkpatrick remained on the observation platform all night, riding there all the way to Kansas City, but no signals were observed.

Upon arrival at Kansas City, Kirkpatrick and Catlett proceeded to the Muehlebach Hotel. Kirkpatrick registered under the name of E. E. Kincaid and waited in his room, where he received a telegram from Tulsa, Oklahoma, as follows:

"Owing to unavoidable incident unable to keep appointed. Will phone you about six. Signed, C. H. Moore."

About 5:30 p.m., on Sunday, July 30, Kirkpatrick received a telephone call from a party who asked if this was "Mr. Kincaid," and upon being advised that it was stated, "This is Moore. You got my telegram?" to which Kirkpatrick replied in the affirmative. Kirkpatrick was then instructed to leave the Muehlebach Hotel in a taxicab and proceed to the LaSalle Hotel and walk west a block or two. He requested permission to be accompanied by a friend, which request was curtly refused. Accordingly, Kirkpatrick took the bag containing the $200,000, arriving at the LaSalle Hotel at about 6 p.m. He walked west. After proceeding no more than half a block, he observed a man approaching him who, upon reaching Kirkpatrick, said, "Mr. Kincaid, I will take that bag," and reached out and took it. Kirkpatrick then stated, "I want some instructions. I must telephone someone who is very interested immediately." The man who had taken the bag told Kirkpatrick to return to the hotel and Urschel would be returned within the specified time. Kirkpatrick then returned to the hotel and from there, proceeded to Oklahoma City. Catlett returned to Tulsa.

Urschel Returns Home

Urschel arrived home exhausted at about 11:30 p.m., July 31, stating that he had been able to sleep but very little during the nine days he had been held in captivity. As soon as he recovered from the shock and regained his strength, he was interviewed by FBI special agents. A detailed statement was obtained including every movement and action taken by himself, the kidnappers, and those with whom they came in contact during his period of captivity.

Urschel's statement concerning the kidnapping and transactions that occurred immediately thereafter was substantially the same as Jarrett's recollection. Urschel stated that immediately after Jarrett's release one of the men produced some cotton, a short bandage, and adhesive tape, and he was blind-folded. Approximately one hour after being blindfolded, the car passed through either two small oil fields or the end of two large fields approximately 30 minutes driving time apart. He could smell the gas and hear the oil pumps working. The first stop was made about 3:30 a.m., when he was taken from the car into the brush by one of the abductors, while the other man was gone approximately 15 minutes after gasoline. About one hour later, a stop was made to open a gate, and approximately three minutes later, another stop was made and another gate opened. Within a minute after the last gate, the car drove into what he took to be a garage. In this building, the men, from their movements and actions, transferred license plates from the Chevrolet sedan to a larger car, which Urschel believed to be a seven-passenger Cadillac or Buick. A berth had been made up in the back of this car and he was told to lie on this bunk. They left this place immediately and after a drive of two or three hours, a stop was made at a filling station, where a woman attendant filled the car with gas. Urschel overheard one of the men asking the woman about crop conditions and she replied that, "The crops around here are burned up, although we may make some broom corn."

Urschel stated that about 9 or 10 a.m., it rained and the road became very slippery, to the extent that on one occasion one of the men was compelled to alight and push the car. In his opinion, at no time on this trip did they drive on pavement. At the next stop, the car was driven directly into what he considered a garage, and at this point, he asked one of the men the time and he replied that it was 2:30 p.m. They remained in this building until dark, when he was taken outside. They passed through a narrow gate and proceeded on a boardwalk. He was led into a house and into a room where he was told there were two beds. The bed he occupied was apparently an iron cot and one of them occupied the other. Shortly after entering this house, he heard the voices of a man and woman in an adjoining room. He stated that his ears were filled with cotton and adhesive tape was placed over them.

Urschel stated that he stayed in this house until the next day—July 24—when he was taken in an automobile by the two men to a house about 15 minutes driving distance. While in the first house, he ate from a small table and he heard barnyard animals outside.

Upon entering the second house, he was led into a room where he was told to lie upon some blankets in a corner of the room. He also heard voices of a man and a woman in the adjoining room which did not resemble the voice of either of the two men who abducted him. Shortly thereafter, this man and woman left the place.

Urschel stated that on the first night, at the second house, a handcuff was placed on one of his wrists and attached to a chair. Next morning, the two men brought up the matter of a contact. They asked Urschel if he had a friend in Tulsa, Oklahoma, who could be trusted, and he suggested the name of John G. Catlett. The men instructed him to write a letter to Catlett and he did.

In addition to the two men who kidnapped him, Urschel was guarded by an old man and a younger man. Urschel stated that, during the time he was held in captivity, one of his two kidnappers discussed freely with him the fact that the had been stealing for 25 years, mentioning Bonnie and Clyde, referring to them as, "Just a couple of cheap filling station and car thieves," and stating that his group did not deal in anything cheap. He also freely discussed a number of bank robberies, advising that he and his friend had been invited to participate in a bank robbery at Clinton, Iowa, but after making a survey of the place, they did not take part in the robbery because the chances of making a "get-away" were unfavorable.

Urschel stated that one of the two kidnappers returned to the house on Friday and brought with him a chain. Thereafter, this chain was attached to his handcuffs, which enabled him to move about to some extent. He observed chickens, cows, and hogs around the place, and he was advised by one of the guards that the had four milk cows. Urschel stated that he was given water in an old tin cup. The well from which this water was obtained was northwest of the house, and the water was obtained from the well by a rope and bucket on a pulley, which made considerable noise. He stated that each morning and evening a plane passed regularly over the house. He managed to get a look at his watch and determined that the morning plane would always pass at approximately 9:45 and the evening plane would pass at approximately 5:45. On Sunday, July 30, when it rained very hard, the morning plane did not pass.

Urschel stated that on Monday, July 31, at about 2:00 p.m., one of his kidnappers returned and told him that he was going to be released, that they had to leave at a certain time, and that another car was going ahead as a pilot car. He was then driven to a point near Norman, Oklahoma, where he was given $10 and released.

The Investigation

While no effort was made by the Bureau to apprehend the kidnappers until after the release of Urschel, extensive investigation was being conducted throughout the United States.

As early as July 24, two days after Urschel was kidnapped, information was obtained at Fort Worth, Texas, indicating the probability that George R. and Kathryn Thorne Kelly were involved in this crime. Consequently, an exhaustive investigation was commenced concerning the history and whereabouts of these individuals. It disclosed that Kathryn Thorne Kelly was the daughter of James Emory Brooks and Mrs. Ora L. Shannon; that Kathryn's mother had divorced Brooks and later married Lonnie Fry at Asher, Oklahoma, and had a daughter, Pauline Fry, now 14 years of age; that Kathryn and Fry were divorced soon after their marriage and she married Charlie Thorne of Coleman, Texas; that Thorne was later found dead under mysterious circumstances pronounced "suicide" by the coroner; and that after Thorne's death a note was found which read, "I cannot live with her or without her." The investigation also disclosed that after Thorne's death Kathryn married George Kelly Barnes, under the name of George R. Kelly. He had served a sentence in the New Mexico State Prison and was known to be enjoying many luxuries, including high-powered automobiles and expensive jewelry, without any visible means of support.

Kelly was born in Tennessee in 1897 and spent his early years in modest surroundings. He attended public schools before becoming a salesman and, later, a bootlegger. He married Kathryn Thorne in 1927. She encouraged Kelly to become deeply involved in a life of crime, bought him a machine gun, and gave him the nickname, "Machine Gun." He concentrated on running illegal alcohol and also robber some banks prior to the Urschel kidnapping.

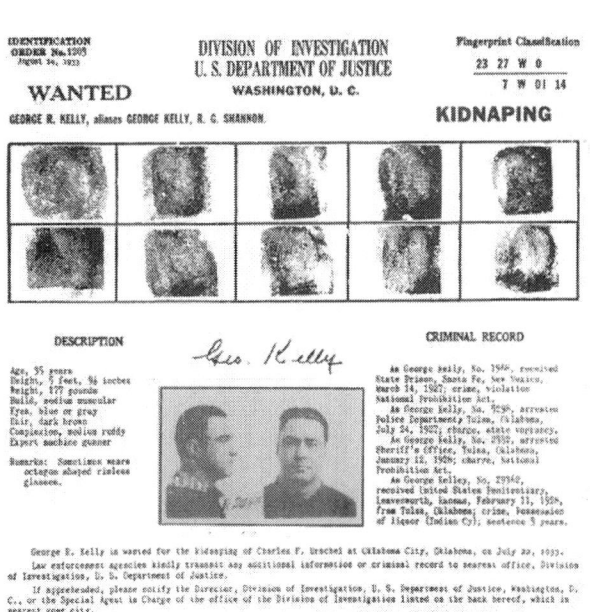

After Urschel was debriefed, the Bureau's activities centered on locating the houses in which Urschel was held and bringing about the apprehension and conviction of the kidnappers. It appeared from the information submitted by Urschel that the best possible clue as to the location of these houses was his statement concerning the weather conditions and the fact that airplanes flew over one of the houses at approximately 9:45 a.m. and 5:45 p.m. daily.

Accordingly, a review was made of all airplane schedules within a radius of 600 miles of Oklahoma City. A check of the Fort Worth-Amarillo Line of American Airways disclosed that a plane left Fort Worth daily at 9:15 a.m. and Amarillo, Texas, at 3:30 p.m. From this information, it was determined that these two planes would be in the vicinity of Paradise, Texas, between 9:40 and 9:45 a.m. and between 5:40 and 5:45 p.m. The daily reports concerning the movements of these planes indicated that from July 23 until July 29, they flew according to schedule; that there was no rain recorded over the route during that period; and that on Sunday, July 30, the plane left Fort Worth at 11:45 a.m., after being detained by a storm, and subsequently, took an extreme northerly course to avoid the storm.

The records of the meteorologist of the United States Weather Bureau of Dallas, Texas were consulted and disclosed that rain was recorded at and in the vicinity of Paradise, Texas, on July 30, 1933; that Paradise and vicinity had an exceedingly dry season; that the first real rain since May 20 in this vicinity was that on July 30; and that the corn began to burn in June.

It will be recalled that the airplane schedules and the weather conditions of Paradise, Texas, corresponded with the weather conditions and airplane schedules Mr. Urschel had noted during his period of captivity. From this information, a check of the suspects who had been under investigation by the Bureau, since the kidnapping of Mr. Urschel, disclosed that Mrs. Shannon, Kathryn Kelly's mother, lived near Paradise.

A closer look at the residence of Mr. and Mrs. R.G. Shannon was needed. Accordingly, a Bureau agent, under a pretext, visited the Shannon residence on August 10, and while there noted the similarity of the house and surroundings with that described by Urschel. It was also determined that R.G. Shannon's son, Armon Shannon, lived on a ranch about a mile and a half from that of his father. An inspection of this house was also made that disclosed a well, a water bucket, a tin cup, a baby's chair, and general surroundings substantially the same as described by Urschel. Further investigation disclosed that Kathryn and George Kelly had been seen in the vicinity during the period in question.

After obtaining the above information, it was decided to raid the Shannon residence in the early morning of August 12. Arrested was Harvey J. Bailey, a notorious criminal and gunman, who had escaped form the Kansas State Penitentiary at Lansing, Kansas, on

May 30, 1933, where he was serving a sentence of 10 to 50 years on a charge of robbing a bank at Fort Scott, Kansas. He also was wanted in connection with the murder of three police officers, an FBI special agent, and their prisoner, Frank Nash, at Kansas City on June 17, 1933. Robert G. Shannon, his wife, Ora L. Shannon, and Armon Shannon were also taken into custody. Bailey had beside him at the time of his arrest a machine gun and two automatic pistols. He was captured before he had an opportunity to use any of these arms. On his person was discovered $1,100, $700 of which was promptly identified as the money used in the payment of ransom for Urschel's release. Subsequent investigation developed that this machine gun had previously been purchased at Fort Worth, Texas, by Kathryn Kelly.

Urschel viewed the residence of the Shannons and immediately identified the house of R.G. Shannon as the house in which he was first held, and that of Armon Shannon as the house in which he was held until his release. Urschel also identified R.G. Shannon and his son, Armon Shannon, as the individuals who stood guard over him during the absence of the two kidnappers. He was able to identify many things, including the men by their voices, the residences by the number of steps which he had taken to enter same, the baby's chair, the galvanized bucket, the tin cup, the squeaking well, the mineral taste of the water, the fowls and animals around the houses, and the chain to which he had been handcuffed.

The Shannons were questioned thoroughly and readily admitted that Urschel had been held at their residences and that they stood guard over him. They advised that Urschel was kidnapped by George Kelly and Albert L. Bates.

Bates, a hardened criminal with a lengthy criminal record, was taken into custody at Denver, Colorado on August 12, 1933, on a local charge. At the time of his arrest, he had in his possession $660, later identified by Bureau agents as part of the Urschel ransom money. He also had a machine gun.

The serial numbers of the ransom bills had been circulated to banks throughout the United States and a number of these bills had been exchanged at the Hennepin State Bank at Minneapolis, Minnesota. Investigation there disclosed that Sam Frederick, a truck driver of Wolk Transfer Company, had presented $1,000 of the ransom money to that bank. Frederick was immediately located and revealed that on August 5, 1933, his boss, Charles Wolk, requested him to accompany two unknown men to the bank, where he obtained a cashier's check under the name of S. H. Peters, in the amount of $1,800, which he immediately gave to the two unknown individuals.

Wolk, upon interview, stated on August 5, he received a telephone call from a person known to him as "Barney," who requested him to get a cashier's check from a bank for $1,800. Subsequent to this call, "Barney," with an unknown individual, came to his office and requested that he accompany them to the bank for the purpose of obtaining a cashier's check. Wolk stated that the did not go with them but sent his driver, Sam Frederick.

It later developed that the cashier's check had been presented for payment by Peter Valder, who upon interview, advised that he was well acquainted with Barney Berman and that on August 2, Berman gave him a check for $1,000 drawn on a bank in Fargo, North Dakota, with the request that he cash the same, which he did. On August 5, the First National Bank and Trust Company of Minneapolis called Wolk and advised him that this check had been returned marked, "insufficient funds." He then advised Berman who, subsequently, gave him a cashier's check drawn to the order of S.H. Peters on the Hennepin State Bank of Minneapolis in the amount of $1,800 and requested him to take out the $1,000 check which had been marked "insufficient funds" and to get the balance of $800 in $100 bills.

It was also discovered that on August 7, 1933, $500 of the Urschel ransom money was deposited in the First National Bank at Minneapolis by Sam Kronick. He was later located and he advised that he obtained this money from his cousin, Sam Kozberg, on August 5. Sam Kozberg was later taken into custody and he advised that on August 5, Barney Berman, at his request, gave him the 25 $20 bills, totaling $500, which he had deposited.

Edward Barney Berman was later interviewed and he advised that on August 3, 1933, he was approached by a man who gave his name as "Collings" and stated that he wanted to buy some liquor. Berman referred him to his associate, "Kid" Cann, who sold Collins 125 cases of whiskey for $5,500 which was paid in bills, a number of which were of the $20 denomination and which had been identified as part of the Urschel ransom money. Berman admitted that he had accompanied Sam Frederick to the Hennepin State Bank and purchased the cashier's check for $1,800. He stated he was accompanied by Clifford Skelly.

Berman's associate, referred to as "Kid" Cann, was later identified as Isadore Blumenfeld, who advised that on August 3, 1933, a man came into their office at the West Hotel in Minneapolis and talked to Barney Berman, who referred this individual, known as Collins, to him. Blumenfeld consummated the deal for 125 cases of whiskey for $5,500 with Collins and turned over the money to another associate, Clifford Skelly. Skelly, upon interview, told the same story as that of Blumenfeld and Berman.

The above-named individuals, together with the parties arrested at Paradise, Texas, Albert Bates, George R. and Kathryn Thorne Kelly, were indicted at Oklahoma City, Oklahoma on August 23, 1933, on a charge of conspiracy to kidnap Charles F. Urschel. All were in custody except the Kellys. On September 30, the jury returned a verdict of guilty against R.G. Shannon, Ora L. Shannon, Armon Shannon, Albert L. Bates, Harvey J. Bailey, Clifford Skelly, and Barney Berman and a verdict of not guilty against Isador Blumenfeld, Sam Kozberg, and Sam Kronick. Peter Valder and Charles Albert Wolk had previously been discharged by virtue of a demurrer to the indictment against them being sustained. On October 7, 1933, Harvey J. Bailey, Albert L. Bates, R.G. Shannon, and Ora L. Shannon were each sentenced to life imprisonment, Armon Shannon to 10 years probation. Edward Barney Berman and Clifford Skelly were each sentenced to serve 5 years.

On September 4, 1933, Harvey J. Bailey, arrested on the Shannon ranch on August 12 and who had previously escaped from the Kansas State Penitentiary, escaped from the Dallas County Jail at about 7:10 a.m. An examination of Bailey's cell, located on the tenth floor of the jail, disclosed that he had escaped by removing three bars from his cell by means of hacksaws which had been smuggled to him together with a revolver. Bailey's freedom, however, was short as he was taken into custody on the afternoon of the same day of escape at Ardmore, Oklahoma.

Investigation disclosed that the hacksaws and revolver were smuggled in to Bailey by Thomas L. Manion, a deputy sheriff and jailer at the Dallas County Jail, and that one Groover C. Bevill of Dallas, Texas, had purchased the hacksaws and assisted Manion in making it possible for Bailey to escape. For this offense Manion and Bevill were indicted at Dallas, Texas on September 25, 1933, and tried and convicted on October 5. Manion was sentenced on October 7 to pay a fine of $10,000 and to serve two years in the United States Penitentiary at Leavenworth. Bevill was sentenced to serve 14 months in the same institution.

While the Bureau was collecting evidence for the trial of Harvey J. Bailey, et al, at Oklahoma City, and for the trial of Manion and Bevill at Dallas, Texas, it was also pursuing efforts to apprehend George and Kathryn Kelly. During the trial at Oklahoma City, the Kellys sent a number of threatening letters to Urschel and Joseph B. Keeyan, Assistant Attorney General, who was in charge of the prosecution at Oklahoma City, threatening their lives and intimidating government witnesses.

The Kellys Are Captured

An investigation conducted at Memphis disclosed that the Kellys were living at the residence of J.C. Tichenor. Special agents from Birmingham, Alabama were immediately dispatched to Memphis, where, in the early morning hours of September 26, 1933, a raid was conducted. George and Kathryn Kelly were taken into custody by FBI agents and Memphis police. Caught without a weapon, George Kelly allegedly cried, "Don't shoot, G-Men! Don't shoot, G-Men!" as he surrendered to FBI agents. The term, which had applied to all federal investigators, became synonymous with FBI agents. The couple was immediately removed to Oklahoma City.

On October 12, 1933, George and Kathryn Kelly were convicted and sentenced to life imprisonment.

Investigation at Coleman, Texas disclosed that the Kellys had been housed and protected by Cassey Earl Coleman and Will Casey and that Coleman had assisted George Kelly in storing $73,250 of the Urschel ransom money on his ranch. This money was located by Bureau agents in the early morning hours of September 27 in a cotton patch on Coleman's ranch. They were both indicted at

Dallas, Texas on October 4, 1933, charged with harboring a fugitive and conspiracy, and on October 17, 1933, Coleman, after entering a plea of guilty, was sentenced to serve one year and one day, and Casey after trial and conviction, was sentenced to serve two years in the United States Penitentiary at Leavenworth, Kansas.

J.C. Tichemor and Langford Ramsey were indicted at Jackson, Tennessee, on charges of conspiracy and harboring and concealing a fugitive, for their part in concealing the Kellys at Memphis, Tennessee. On October 21, 1933, they were each sentenced to serve two years and six months imprisonment.

Investigation also disclosed that while the Kellys were in Chicago, Illinois, they were shielded by Abe and Charles Kaplan.

During the time in which Urschel was being held a kidnap victim, Kathryn Kelly maintained a residence at Fort Worth, Texas. She had been living with Louise Magness. Shortly after the payment of the ransom money, and in response to a telegram, Louise Magness flew from Fort Worth, Texas to Des Moines, Iowa, where she joined George and Kathryn Kelly. She then drove the Kellys to Brownwood, Texas and posing as the sister of George Kelly, purchased for Kelly and his wife a 1928 Chevrolet sedan.

On February 22, 1934, Magness was indicted at Fort Worth, Texas, charged with harboring George and Kathryn Kelly. On April 30, 1934, she entered a plea of guilty and was sentenced to serve one year and one day in the Federal Industrial Institution for Women at Alderson, West Virginia.

Investigation disclosed that Albert Bates had married Mrs. Clara Feldman, who had a son, Edward George Feldman. Clara Feldman had a brother-in-law, Alvin H. Scott, who was also a close associate of the above-mentioned parties. After the Urschel kidnapping, Bates joined Clara and Edward Feldman in Denver, Colorado, and later visited relatives in Portland, Oregon. Bates then returned to Denver, Colorado, where he was arrested shortly thereafter.

Clara and Edward Feldman had no knowledge of Bates' arrest until a prisoner, who had recently been released from the county jail in Denver, left a message at the Feldman apartment to the effect that Bates was in custody and that Clara Feldman should "look in the suitcase." The suitcase was found to be filled with $20 bills. Clara and Edward Feldman then proceeded to Cheyenne, Wyoming, where they buried this money.

Shortly thereafter, Ben Laska, a Denver attorney, communicated with the Feldmans, advised them that he was defending Bates and that he would get in touch with them when he needed some money. Laska then took from Edward Feldman all identifying papers and told Feldman to use the fictitious name of Axel C. Johnson. Laska advised Edward and Clara Feldman to go east and live in large cities where their identities would not become known. Thereafter, at Laska's request, Clara and Edward Feldman paid Laska $8,000 of this ransom money to cover his expenses in the defense of Bates. Laska then asked for a diagram of the place where the remaining ransom money was buried. Edward Feldman furnished him with a fictitious diagram.

Laska subsequently demanded of Edward Feldman an additional $2,000. By prearrangement, Edward Feldman met Laska at Oklahoma City, Oklahoma, where $2,000 of the Urschel ransom money was delivered to Laska.

On December 4, 1934, Clara Feldman advised special agents of the location of additional ransom currency in the sum of $38,460 which had been cached away. On November 2, 1934, Alvin H. Scott, a brother-in-law of Clara Feldman was seriously injured in an automobile accident at Roseburg, Oregon. At the time of this accident, Scott had in his possession $1,360 in Urschel ransom money. A search of the premises of Alvin Scott disclosed the location of an additional sum of $6,140 in Urschel ransom money.

Clara Feldman and Edward Feldman were taken into custody at Dunsmuir, California, November 9, 1934, $1,100 in ransom money being recovered from their possession. Immediate questioning of them by special agents disclosed the location of $1,520 additional ransom currency which these parties had cached at a point near Woodland, Washington. Continued questioning of Alvin H. Scott disclosed the location of additional ransom money in the sum of $5,000.

On December 14, 1934, the following persons were indicted by a federal grand jury at Oklahoma City, Oklahoma, charging them with conspiracy to violate the Kidnapping Statute: Ben B. Laska, James C. Mathers, Clara Feldman, Edward Feldman, and Alvin Scott. Accordingly, Clara and Edward Feldman and Alvin Scott were removed to Oklahoma City. On December 17, 1934, Ben Laska was taken into custody by agents in Oklahoma City. It was alleged that Mathers had accepted from Laska $2,000 of the Urschel ransom money, with knowledge of the character of the money.

On December 17, 1934, Clara Feldman entered a plea of guilty to the indictment. Edward Feldman and Alvin Scott pleaded guilty on January 2, 1935. Alvin Scott, Clara Feldman, and Edward Feldman were sentenced on June 15, 1935, to serve five years each in a federal penitentiary. These sentences were suspended for five years, and each was placed on probation.

James C. Mathers and Ben Laska were tried in federal court at Oklahoma City, Oklahoma, on June 10, 1935. On June 14, 1935, Mathers was acquitted by a directed verdict. On June 15, 1935, Laska was sentenced to serve 10 years in a federal penitentiary.

Laska was released on a $10,000 bond pending an appeal. The U.S. Circuit Court of Appeals for the 10th Circuit at Denver, Colorado on March 27, 1936 rendered a decision affirming the District Court at Oklahoma City, Oklahoma. Laska surrendered to the U.S. marshal at Oklahoma City, Oklahoma on August 1, 1936 and was removed to the U.S. Penitentiary at Leavenworth, Kansas, on the same date.

Mrs. Mollie O. Bert, a Denver, Colorado attorney, furnished some untruthful testimony during the trials of Laska. As a result of this testimony, a complaint filed against Mrs. Bert at Oklahoma City, Oklahoma on June 15, 1936, charging her with perjury. She was released on a $5,000 bond after a plea of not guilty.

On October 1, 1936, Mrs. Bert withdrew her plea of not guilty and entered a plea of nolle contendere and was sentenced on the same date to serve one year and one day imprisonment, which sentence was suspended pending good behavior for one year.

Twenty-one persons were convicted in this case, the sentences including six life sentences and other sentences total 58 years, two months, and three days.

George "Machine Gun" Kelly died of a heart attack at the Federal Penitentiary, Leavenworth, Kansas, on July 17, 1954. Kathryn Kelly was released from prison in Cincinnati in 1958; she was last known to be residing in Oklahoma.

Printed in Great Britain
by Amazon

53945211R00059